From My Heart

Art Therapy

by

Daphne E. Jessie-Walker

Dorrance Publishing Co
585 Alpha Drive
Suite 103
Pittsburgh, PA 15238
Visit our website at *www.dorrancebookstore.com*

ISBN: 979-8-89027-219-5
eISBN: 979-8-89027-717-6

INVISIBLE SCARS

On The Outside I Smile And Laugh For The Joys Of Life Extended To Me
I Stand Proudly Proclaiming All The Love You Gladly Show For Me
I Cry In Awe Of The Miracles Performed In My Life
I Dance In Praise To Honor You For All That You Do

But People Don't Understand Why I Am In What They See Of Me
They Can't See The Secrets That's Embedded Deep Within My Soul
They Don't Know Of How Our Relationship Of Love Takes Hold
They Don't Understand That My Faith In You Is Stronger Than What They Know

They Can't See All Of My Scars Because They're Invisible
And For That I Am Grateful That I Don't Look Like All That I've Been Through
They Don't Know That The Armor That I Wear In Battle Is Not The Same I Wear For Show

So They Don't Know About The Invisible Scars That I Bear Inside Of Me

I Can Share The Stories Of All The Battles That You've Fought Right Beside Of Me
Of All The Times You've Shielded Me From The Hurricane Winds Blowing All Around Me
The Stories Of How You Mended My Wounds From The Fiery Darts That Struck Me
And How You Restored Strength In Me And Given Me Victory Regardless Of How It Seems

Still People Don't Understand Why I Am In What They See Of Me
They Can't See The Secrets That's Embedded Deep Within My Soul

They Don't Know Of How Our Relationship Of Love Takes Hold
They Don't Understand That My Faith In You Is Stronger Than What
They Know

They Can't See All My Scars Because They're Invisible
And For That I Am Grateful That I Don't Look Like All The Things That
I've Been Through
But They Don't Know Because The Armor That I Wear In Battle Is Not
The Same I Wear For Show

So How Can They Know About The Invisible Scars That I Bear Inside Of Me

Do I Show Them Just How Warn And Battered The Armor That I Wear?
Do I Share How The Darts Struck Through All Of The Weaknesses In My Life?
Do I Tell Them The Errors Of My Ways? And All The Mistakes That I Made?
Or How These Scars Are The Thorns In My Life That I Alone Have To Bear?

So People Don't Understand Why I Am In What They See Of Me
They Can't See The Secrets That Are Embedded Deep Within My Soul
They Don't Know Of How Our Relationship Of Love Takes Hold
They Don't Understand That My Faith In You Is Stronger Than What
They Know

That Is Why They Can't See All My Scars Because They're Invisible
And For That I Am Grateful That I Don't Look Like All The Things That
I've Been Through
So They Can't Know That The Armor That I Wear In Battle Is Not The
Same I Wear For Show

So They Just Don't Know About The Invisible Scars That I Bear Inside Of Me

I'll Just Tell Them How You Took Me By My Hands
How You Washed Me Clean, Mended My Open Wounds, And Made Them
Invisible
Because They Are The Invisible Scars That I Bear Inside Of Me

THE SHROUD

When You Look At The Shroud Is It Possible To See, The Bloodstained
Face Of Religion's Controversy?
Can You See The Wounds That Tells How He Suffered, The Torture He
Experienced By The Hands Of Another
For Our Sins, Our Iniquities And All Of Our Transgressions?
He Laid Down His Life, So We Can Proclaim That We Are Saved By His
Blood And We Are Healed By His Stripes
He Arose And Now Sits On The Throne Next To God, And He Left In
That Empty Tomb His Bloodstained Face On The Shroud

JESUS

I Believe That In The Name Of Jesus, If You Pray In The Precious Name Of Jesus
That Is The Answer, That Is The Way To God In Prayer

I Believe That There Is No Other Answer, That There Is No Other Way
But To Live As Christ Jesus, Learn All Of His Ways To Go To God In Prayer

Love The Name Of Jesus Christ, Love The Son Of God And His Sacrifice
Worship Him, Then Glorify Him In Service, In Honor, And In Prayer

Call On Him In Charity, Call On Him In Love, Call On Him In Prayer To Amplify Your Voice, Let God Hear Your Heart

Call On Him In Intercession, Call On Him In Declaration, Call On Him In Adoration Of His Love, So Pure, Let God Hear Your Voice

Let God Hear Your Prayers In The Name Of Jesus, In The Precious Name Of Jesus Christ

When You Call On Him, Believe In Him, And Stand On The Word That He Gave To You
Believe The Words Of The Lord Is Right, Let Him See Your Light When You Pray

Trust In Him, Have Faith In Him Knowing That God Has A Plan
Then God Will Work The Plans For You, He'll Light The Path For You To Take

Trust In The Lord With Your Whole Being, There's Nothing He Won't Do For You
Believe Jesus Intercedes For You, When You Humble Your Heart In Prayer

Call On Him In Charity, Call On Him In Love, Call On Him In Prayer To Amplify Your Voice, Let God Hear Your Heart

Call On Him In Intercession, Call On Him In Declaration, Call On Him In Adoration Of His Love, So Pure, Let God Hear Your Voice

Let God Hear Your Prayers In The Name Of Jesus, In The Precious Name Of Jesus Christ

CALL ON HIM

Call On Him
He's Waiting For You To Call On Him
He Wants To Heal Your Body
He Wants To Heal Your Mind
So, Call On Him

Call On Him
He Wants To Hold Your Hands
He Wants To Rock You In His Arms
He Wants To Keep You Close And Safe
So, Call On Him

Call On Him
No Matter What The Problem Is
No Matter What You're Going Through
No Matter What Your Plight
Just Call On Him

Call On Him
He Wants To Wipe Your Tears Away
He Will See You Through
He Wants You To Know That It's Going To Be Okay
Just Call On Him

Call On Him
He Will Make It Right
He Has A Plan For You
There's Nothing That's Impossible For Him
So, Simply Call On Him

Call On Him
No Matter The Name That You Call Him
Just Call On Him
Cause He's The Same God
Oh, Just Call On The Names Of God
Call On The Name Of Jesus
Call On The Holy Spirit

Just Call On Him

HOLY SPIRIT

I'm Calling On You Now, Yeah
Right Now, For You Holy Spirit
Holy Spirit—Holy Spirit, Reign Down On Me

I'm Calling On You Now, Yeah
Right Now, For You Holy Spirit
Holy Spirit—Holy Spirit, Consume Me Now

I'm Calling On You Now, Yeah
Right Now, For You To Enter In
Enter In Holy Spirit, Enter In

I'm Calling On You Now, Yeah
Right Now, For You To Rain On Me
Rain On Me Holy Spirit, Rain On Me

I'm Calling On You Now, Yeah
Right Now, For You To Touch Me
Touch Me Holy Spirit, Touch Me

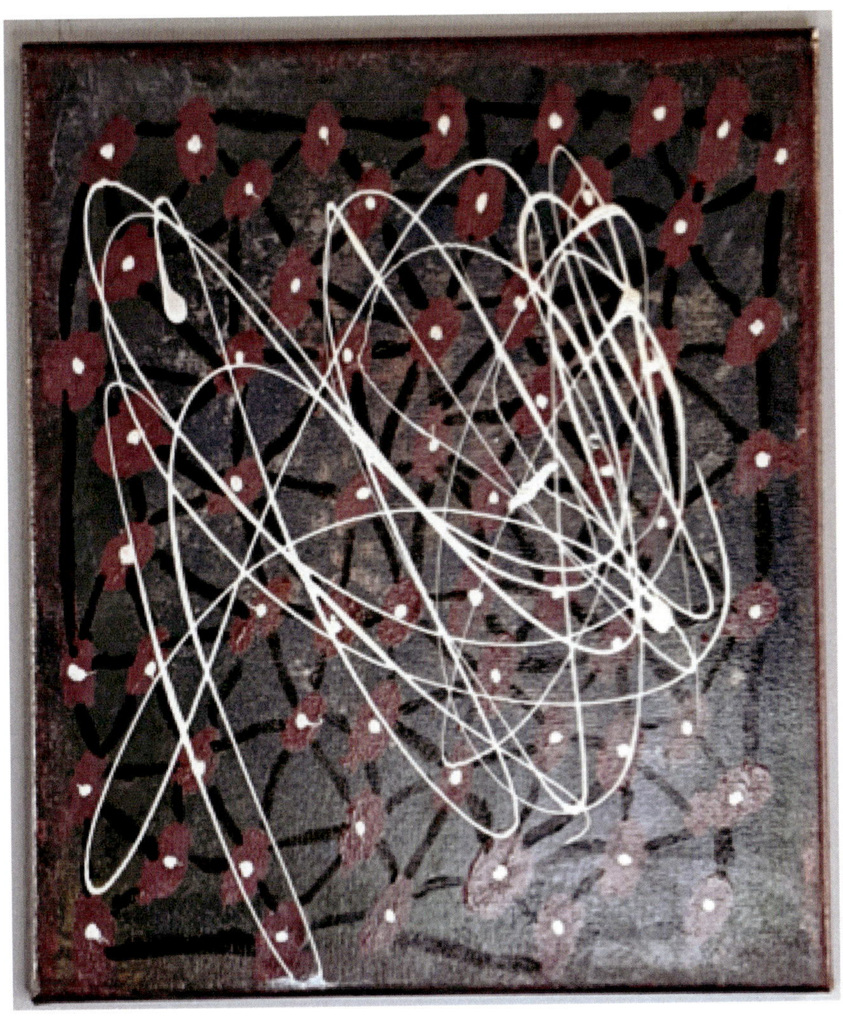

Thorn In My Flesh

Lord, I'm Pleading With You To Remove This Thorn In My Flesh
God, Help Me Please, Remove This Thorn In My Flesh
It's Trying Hard To Kill Me, To Destroy My Mortal Soul, Tormenting Me
And It's Making Me Weak

Oh, Help Me Please, I'm In Need Of Your Help
Help Me Please, Lord, I'm In Need Of Your Strength
Oh God, Please

I Know That Your Grace Is Sufficient For Me
With All Your Loving Kindness, That's That Grace And Mercy Thing
For Your Strength Is Made Perfect In My Weaknesses And In That Way
When I Am Weak, I Am Stronger Than I Know

But This Thing Is Hurting Me, Hindering Me, And Right Now I Am Weak
That's Why My Human Mortal Soul Is Pleading To You, God
Oh Lord, I'm Pleading With You To Remove This Thorn In My Flesh

God, Help Me Please, Remove This Thorn In My Flesh
It's Trying Hard To Kill Me, To Destroy My Mortal Soul, Tormenting Me
And It's Making Me Weak

God, Help Me Please, I'm In Need Of Your Help
Help Me—Help Me, Please, I'm In Need Of Your Strength
Oh God, Please—Please—Please, Please

Remove, This Thorn
Remove, This Thorn In My Flesh
God, Please

HOLD ME

Lord, My Heart Is Shattered Into Pieces
And I Just Don't Know What Else To Do
Don't Get Me Wrong, I Still Trust In You
But I'm Surrounded In Darkness And Can't See The Light Of Day

I'm Trying Hard To Keep It Together
To Push Through My Weakness And Through My Pain
But It's Getting Harder And Harder To Move, Lord
I Need You To Hold Me

Hold Me, Not Just My Hand, Hold Me
I Need More Than A Touch From You, Hold Me
Embrace Me, Jesus, Embrace Me Lord, Hold Me
Wrap Your Loving Arms Around Me, Hold Me

I Need To Feel The Beat Of Your Heart
To Feel The Warmth Of Your Blood, Hold Me
Remind Me That Everything Is Gonna Be Alright
I Need You To Hold Me

Please, Hold Me—Hold Me, God, Hold Me

THROUGH THE FIRE

I Am God And I Sent Down
Two Parts Of Me To Be With You
To Comfort And To Open Up Your Eyes

I Sent To You My Son And My Spirit
The Very Parts Of Me
The Essence Of My Being

My Fire That I Sent With Them
Will Teach You, To Show You The Way
And To Help You Understand
The Love That I Have For You
And It Is

Through The Fire I Shall Appear To You
Through The Fire I Will Baptize
Through The Fire I Will Cleanse You
Come Unto Me
There You'll See
The Plans I Have For You

Through The Fire I Shall Make You Whole
Through The Fire I Will Purify
Through The Fire I Will Deliver You
Come Unto Me
There You'll See
The Plans I Have For You

Through The Fire I Shall Guide You

Through The Fire I Will Light The Way
Through The Fire I Will Comfort You
Come Unto Me
There You'll See
The Plans I Have For You

Through The Fire I Shall Protect
Through The Fire I Will Provide
Through The Fire I Will Be With You
Come Unto Me
There You'll See
What I Have In Store For You

Come Unto Me
And There You'll See
The Love That I Have For You

I'm Not Dead

Can You Hear Me Love? Wake Up, I'm Not Dead
Can You See Me Love? Look Up, I'm Not Dead
Can You Feel Me Love? Believe, I'm Not Dead
No, I'm Alive; I'm Alive

I Am Here To Mend The Broken Hearted
I Am Here To Free You Of Your Pain
I Am Here To Heal The Sick And Wounded
Believe Me Love I am Here And Not Dead
Believe Me When I Say I'm Not Dead
I'm Alive

Can You Hear Me Love? Wake Up, I'm Not Dead
Can You See Me Love? Look Up, I'm Not Dead
Can You Feel Me Love? Believe, I'm Not Dead
No, I'm Alive; I'm Alive

I Am Here To Sooth Your Heart Of Sorrow
I Am Here So Lay Down Your Heavy Burdens
Can You Feel My Loving Hands Upon You?
Believe In Your Heart, I'm Not Dead
Take Me By My Hand, My Love, I'm Not Dead
I'm Alive

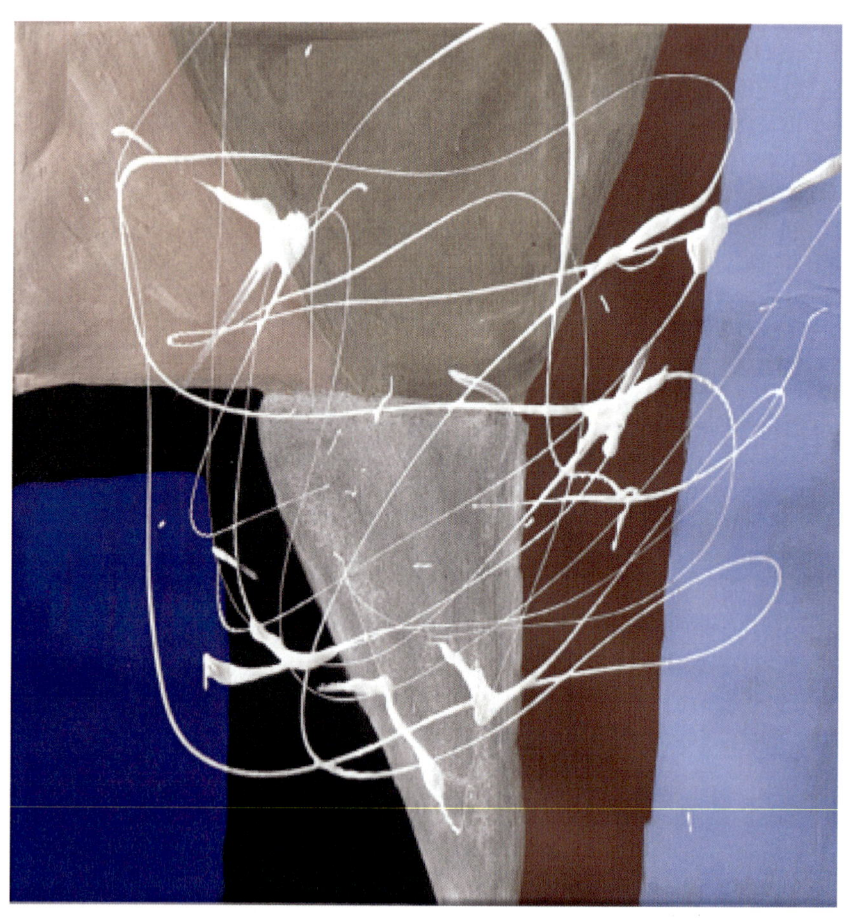

GOD IS NO WAYS DONE

I Know You're Hurt, And I Know That You're Tired
Things Haven't Turned Out For You, In The Way That You Planned
You've Been Through So Many Trials, And You Question If God Is Done
With Using You

But If You Have Breath In Your Body, Then I'm Here To Tell You
No Matter What Is Going On With You, That God Is No Ways Done With
You Yet

I Know That Some People Try To Tell You To Throw In The Towel
Telling You That There's Nothing More On This Earth For You To Do
That Your Mind Is In The Clouds Of An Unachievable Dream, And That
Your Vision Is Nothing More Than A Fantasy

But If God Gave You The Vision, Then Trust And Believe
Knowing That You Know That God Still Has A Plan For You
Cause God Is No Ways Done With You Yet

Your Body May Have Been Riddled With Sickness And Pain
But When God Has A Plan For You No Matter What Life Throws Your Way
He's Not Done With You Yet

I Don't Care What Anybody Else Say, Just Have A Talked With God And
Keep Pressing Your Way, Because The Spirit Of The Living God Said That
He's Not Done With You Yet

God Is No Ways Done With You Yet

YOU CAME TO ME

When I Was Afraid, You Came To Me
When I Was Hurt, You Came To Me
When I Was Lost And Couldn't Find My Way Through The Storm, You Came To Me

Sweet Holy Spirit, Oh, God's Heavenly Dove
Sent Down From The Heavens Out Of Love
You Came To My Rescue And Delivered Me
You Came To Me

When I Was Sick, You Came To Me
When I Was Broken, You Came To Me
When I Was In The Dark And Couldn't See The Light Of Day, You Came To Me

Sweet Holy Spirit, Oh, God's Heavenly Dove
Sent Down From The Heavens Out Of Love
You Came To My Rescue And Delivered Me
You Came To Me

HOLY FIRE

Holy Light, Sent Down From Heaven
With All Your Glory

Marvelous In All Thy Ways, A Manifested Flame
Wash My Soul And Cleanse My Spirit
Make Me White As Snow, Make Me Whole Again

Holy Fire, Out Of The Tomb
You Rose Again

Lighting The Way To Heaven, A Manifested Love
You Shine Upon Us Reigning From Above
With Eternal Life As Promised In His Word

Hallelujah, Blessed Fire
Hallelujah, Holy Fire
Hallelujah,
All Hail The Powerful Might Of God's Majesty

Oh Holy Fire, Holy Light
Come Shine Your Glorious Light Again On Thee

ONE STEP AT A TIME

In This Life, This Journey
The Challenges That I Faced To Test My Faith
Has Turned My World Upside Down

Situations Caused Me To Cry And Scream
"Why Lord... How Could This Be?"

I Know That I'm Not Perfect
But I Try My Best To Live Right
In Spite Of The Temptations That I Face
And The Mistakes That I Make

But Because My Faith And My Trust Is In You
I Pray For Peace In My Soul And Strength In My Heart
As I Rise From My Knees To Press My Way Through

Lord, I'm Taking It

One Step At A Time, Day By Day
Make No Mistake, I'm Gonna Finish This Race
This Path Laid Out Before Me May Be Hard For Some To Conceive
But It's Designed By One Higher Than I

One Step At A Time, Day By Day
God Has Made A Way For Me To Take
For He Knows What's Best For Me, Even Though Times I Cannot See It
But I Trust And Believe And Let Him Take The Lead

Step By Step, He Lit My Path, He Has A Plan, For Me To Succeed
I Can't Stop, No Matter What, May Come My Way, Cause In The End
I Will Win If I Keep My Eyes On Him

One Step At A Time, Day By Day
Make No Mistake, I'm Gonna Finish This Race
By Taking It One Step At A Time, No Matter How Long It Takes

God Has Made A Way, For Me To Take

I Can Hear The Angels Say
"Take One Step At A Time
Your Path Is By Design
You'll Finish Right On Time
Day By Day
Day By Day"

Yeah, I Got This

LIFE'S JOURNEY

Oh Lord, I Have Been Through So Many Trials, I Can't See Past This
Storm, You Have To Help Me Understand
Please Tell Me What's Going On

I Know That You Have A Better Plan Designed Especially For Me To
Achieve And To Glorify Your Name
So I Surrender Unto Your Will

You Know The Best Path For Me, You've Already Paved The Way
So I'll Just Trust And Believe As You Light My Way
Through This Journey I Have To Take

To Walk In The Promises You Said And Prosperity Decreed
Will Take For Me To Act On My Faith
And To Be A Doer Of Your Word

Because I Seek First The Kingdom Of God And I Follow In Your Life Displayed
I Have To Remain Strong
No Matter What Comes My Way

You Know The Best Path For Me, You've Already Paved The Way
So I'll Just Trust And Believe As You Light My Way
Through This Journey I Have To Take

No Matter How Rough The Road Gets, I Can Still Thrive
I Can Face Every Trial With You By My Side
I Don't Have To Worry Because It Says In Your Word
That You're The Light Unto My Pathway And The Lamp To My Feet
And If I Cast My Cares Upon You I Cannot Be Defeated

For You Know
You Know The Best Path For Me, You've Already Paved The Way
So I'll Just Trust And Believe As You Light My Way
Through This Journey I Have To Take

Oh It's My Life's Journey, This Journey I Have To Take

TAKE THE TIME

Love, Got A Minute? Can We Talk?
I Can See God's Spirit Surrounding Your Heart
Even Though You May Fall Throughout The Storm Sometimes, He's Holding You Close In His Arms

Count Your Blessings, His Given Vision Comes With Your Decision To Get Up And Walk
So, When Down Take A Breath, Close Your Eyes, Say A Prayer Because He's There And Say To Yourself

Just Take The Time Out And See What He's Done
Despite Of The Storms Look Up And Look At The Son
Each New Day Is New Life
Each New Day Gives New Grace And New Mercies
Brand New Mercies

With Each Breath You Take Is A Chance To Say
With Your Hands Up Raised, In All Faith In Your Heart
"I Receive Him," Confess That You Trust In Him
And Say, "I Believe God"

Love, Your Still Here, Now Let The Light Within You Guide You From Out Of The Darkness
There's A Work To Complete, A Greater Design He Assigned To You
No Need To Explain It

Count Your Blessings, Don't Be Afraid, This Open Door, No Man Can Close It
So, When Discouraged Take A Breath, Remember There's A Plan
So Go Soar And Say To Yourself

Just Take The Time Out And See What He's Done
Despite Of The Storms Look Up And Look At The Son
Each New Day Is New Life,
Each New Day Gives New Grace And New Mercies
Brand New Mercies

With Each Breath You Take Is A Chance To Say
With Your Hands Up Raised, In All Faith In Your Heart
"I Receive Him," Confess That You Trust In Him
And Say, "I Believe God"

He's Building You, He's Growing You
Each Time The Storm Winds Blow, He's Making You Stronger
Pick Up Your Bed, Get Up! Love, He's Taking You Higher
Higher And Higher

Take The Time Out And See What He's Done
Despite Of The Storms Look Up And Look At The Son
Each New Day Is New Life, Each New Day Gives New Grace And New
Mercies Brand New Mercies

With Each Breath You Take Is A Chance To Say
With Your Hands Up Raised, In All Faith In Your Heart
"I Receive Him," Confess That You Trust In Him
And Say, "I Believe God"

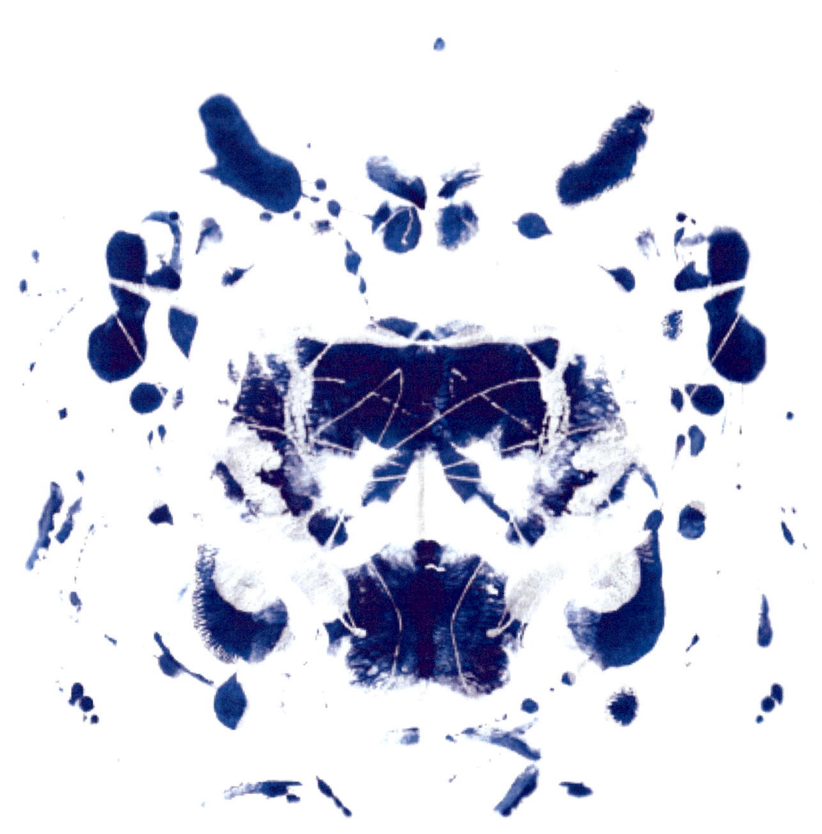

I BELIEVE IN GOD

I Believe In God, Creator Of All Things

I Believe In Him As Jesus Christ, The Son He Sent, To Show His Love For All To See

I Believe In God, The Spirit That's Dwelling With In Me
I Believe In Him My Counselor And Teacher, For He Is Everything That I Need

He Takes The Time To Show Me All That He Is, If I Believe
He Grabs Me And Performs Miracles Out Of His Love For Me

He Restores My Sight Whenever Blinded
And With His Strength, He Makes Me To Walk
He Hears My Cry And Sees My Tears And Always Mends My Broken Heart

I Believe In God, The Ruler Of All Things
I Believe In Him, My Guardian And Keeper, The One Whose Hands Are There Protecting Me

I Believe In God, The Master Who Reigns Over Me
I Believe In Him My Savior, Lord, And King, For He Blew The Breath Of Life In Me

He Takes The Time To Show Me All That He Is, If I Believe
He Grabs Me And Performs Miracles Out Of His Love For Me

He Restores My Sight Whenever Blinded
And With His Strength, He Makes Me To Walk
He Hears My Cry And Sees My Tears And Always Mends My Broken Heart

So I'm Forever Grateful To Him
Thankful For The Things He's Done And All That He Is Doing For Me

I'm Forever Grateful To Him
For The Love He Shares With Me Is More Than I Could Ever Dream

I'm Forever Grateful To Him
Thankful For The Things He's Done And All That He Is Doing For Me

I'm Forever Grateful To Him
For The Love He Shares With Me Is More Than I Could Ever Dream
Of Him To Be

He Saved My Soul And Gave Me New Life; Forgave My Wrongs And
Shown Me The Light

He Has Given Power In My Voice, In My Dance, In My Walk
It's Why I'm So Thankful, Why I Believe In Him; Eternally Grateful

Yes, I'm Forever Grateful To Him
Thankful For The Things He's Done And All That He Is Doing For Me

I'm Forever Grateful To Him
For The Love He Shares With Me Is More Than I Could Ever Dream
Of Him To Be

Oh I Believe, I Believe In God

The One Who Heals Me, The One Who Saves Me, The One Who Lives
Inside Of Me

The One Who Covers Me, Who Sanctifies Me, Forgives And Wash My Sins Away

The One Who Sees Me, The One Who Hears Me, Delivers Me From Endless Pain

Oh I Believe, I Believe In God

He's My Provider And My Protector Who Shields Me From The Storms
And The Rain

He Is My Fortress And My Strong Tower When Enemies Try To Come My Way

For He Loves Me And Cares About Me, The Guide That Leads Me Along
Life's Way

Oh I Believe, I Believe In God

I'm So Thankful For All Of His Love Shown
I Believe In God

He's Oh So Faithful That's Why I'm So Grateful
I Believe In God

He's All Seeing, Most Powerful
That's Why I Believe

He Supplies My Needs And Takes Care Of Me
I Believe In God

He Always Keeps His Hands On Me
I Believe In God

He Loves Me And That's Why I Believe

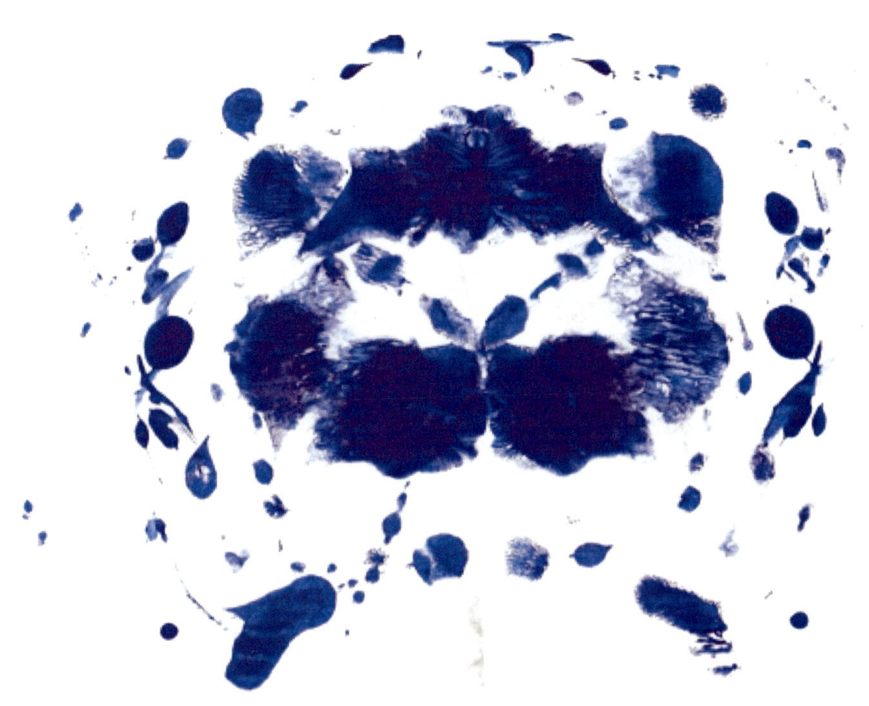

BECAUSE OF HIM

It's Because Of Him I Can Breathe
It's Because Of Him I Can Talk
It's Because Of Him I Can Sing
Of All I've Witnessed Of His Miracles

It's Because Of Him I Can Dance
It's Because Of Him I Can Stand
It's Because Of Him I Can Walk
Through Every Door Closed And Open For Me

It's Because Of Him I Can Dream
It's Because Of Him I Can See
It's Because Of Him That I Believe
In Every Vision That He's Given To Me

It's Because Of Him That I Can Smile
It's Because Of Him I'm Filled With Such Joy
It's Because Of Him I Can Feel
His Holy Spirit Every Time He Is Near

It's Because Of Him That I Have Peace
It's Because Of Him That I'm Free
It's Because Of Him I Can Achieve
Everything That I Dare To Dream In Him

It's Because Of Him That I've Been Healed
It's Because Of Him I'm Still Here
It's Because Of Him I Can Live
To Tell How He Changed Me And Touched My Life

And It's All Because Of Him
Now I Can Truly Say
I've Been Set Free, I'm Still Here
I'm Alive And I Can Live Again
I'm Alive, I'm Alive

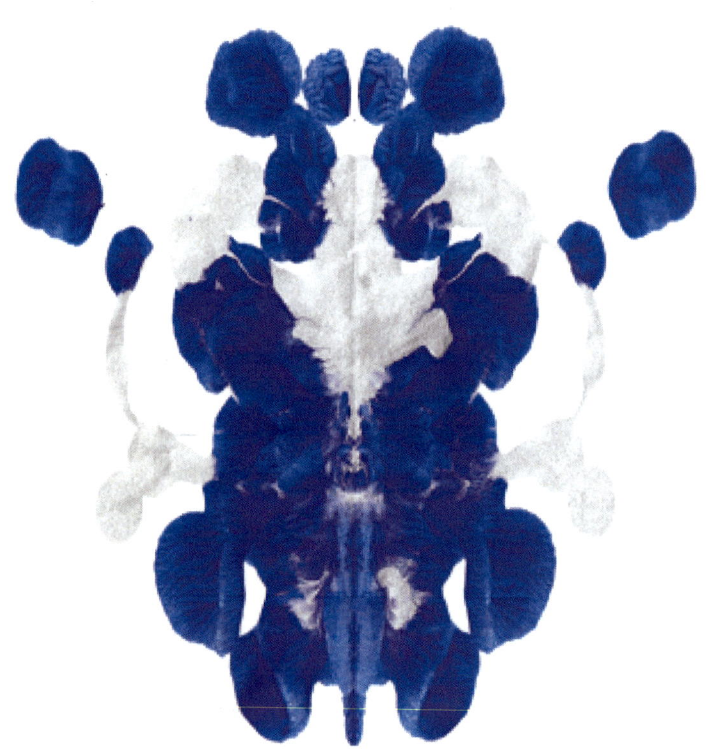

PERCEPTION

How Life Is Perceived By You Through The Windows Of The Soul Will
Always Reveal The Spirit That Is Housed Within You
That You And You Alone Allows To Control Your Every Thought, Your
Every Motivation, And Your Every Move
So, What Do You See? How Do You Perceive What's Right Before Your
Eyes? Can You See Me? What Can You See?

IN THE CLOUDS

I Can Never Forget The Day I Looked Up To The Sky
And I Saw Your Majesty In The Clouds
In Your Glory, I Was So In Awe Of You
I Couldn't Help But Stare At The Marvel You Showed To Me

In The Clouds You Showed Me Your Kingdom
And In The Clouds You Showed Me The Pearly Gates
I See The Many Mansions That's Built Upon The Hills In The Clouds
You Showed Me You

Majestic In All Your Ways
Sometimes It's Hard For Me To Believe
The Love You Have For Me

I'm So In Awe Of You In How You Choose To Show Me You
In The Clouds

I Can Never Forget The Day I Looked Out The Window
As I'm Flying In The Air
The Beauty Of The Earth, You Created
Is Such A Wonderful Sight To See

But Most Of All, The Thing That Has Me In Such Awe Of You
Is That You Showed Me You Upon The Clouds
Standing Tall With Your Arms Open Wide Held Up High
Guiding And Protecting Me, Keeping Me Safe From Harm

Majestic In All Your Ways
Sometimes It's Hard For Me To Believe
The Love You Have For Me

I'm So In Awe Of You In How You Choose To Show Me You
In The Clouds
In The Sky. Up In The Clouds, You Showed Me You

I'm In Awe Of You, In How You Chose To Show Me You
Up In The Clouds
In The Sky, Up High, In The Clouds, You Showed Me You
In The Sky. In The Clouds, You Showed Me You
I'm In Awe Of You
In Awe Of You

I'm In Awe Of You, In How You Chose To Show Your Love
Up In The Clouds
In The Sky, Up High In The Clouds, You Showed Your Love
In The Sky, In The Clouds, You Showed Your Love
I'm In Awe Of You
In Awe Of You

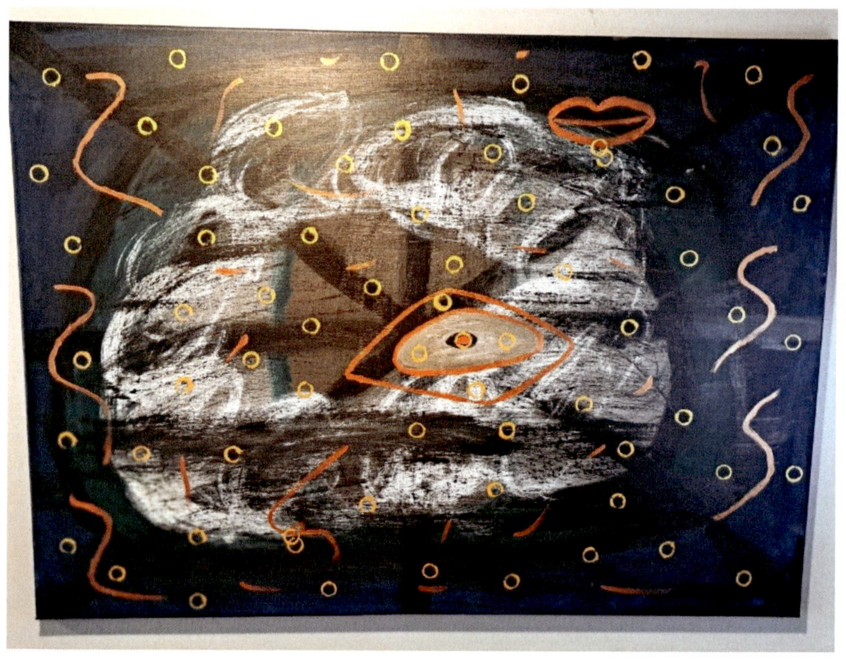

I LONG TO SEE YOU AGAIN

Jesus, I Long To See You Again
Standing Upon The Clouds
Leading My Way Across The Sky

Jesus, I Long To See You Again
Holding Me Safely In Your Arms
Protecting Me From All Harm

I Long To See You Again
As I Look Up To The Sky
Seeking Your Presence

Oh Jesus, I Long To See You Again

Hearing Your Voice As The Angel Sing
Giving Peace To My Soul
Quieting My Fears
In The Mist Of The Storm

Oh Jesus, I Long To See You Again

I Long To See You Again

HUNGER FOR YOU

Bread Of Heaven, You Are The Bread Of Life
You've Sacrificed Your Life, What A Price
For The Words That You've Spoken To My Heart
Shined The Light Of Love For Me When I Was Lost

I Need You That I May Live, To Fulfill My Purpose For My Life
And For Your Perfect Will, Your Will, Not Mine
For You Are The Way To Eternal Life, You Are The Only Way I Choose To Live
Lord, I Hunger For You

I Hunger For Your Love
I Hunger For Your Grace
I Hunger For Your Mercy
And For Righteousness
I Hunger For Your Touch
I Hunger For Your Warm Embrace
I Hunger For Your Word, Your Voice
To See You Face To Face
To Stand In Your Presence
Engulfed In Holiness
Oh, Lord, I Hunger For You

You're The One True Vine, You're The Fruit Of Life
With A Light Of Love So Bright
It Struck My Heart; To Show All The Way To Walk
Out Of The Darkness Into Brighter Days With You By Our Side

I Need You To Help Me Make It Through This Journey Of Life
And To Fulfill My Destiny For Your Plan Not Mine
For You Are The Example For My Life You Are The Way I Choose To Live
I Hunger For You

I Hunger For Your Love
I Hunger For Your Grace
I Hunger For Your Mercy
And For Righteousness
I Hunger For Your Touch
I Hunger For Your Warm Embrace
I Hunger For Your Word, Your Voice
To See You Face To Face
To Stand In Your Presence
Engulfed In Holiness
Oh, Lord, I Hunger For You

Your Word Says Taste And See That The Lord Is Good
How The Sweetness Of Your Word Is Sweeter Than Honey
Yes, It Is Sweeter Than Honey
I Come Unto You, Eternal Manna From Heaven To Be My Strength And
My Guide That I May Make It Through This Life
Never Hungry Or Thirsty For A Life Outside Of You

I Hunger For Your Love
I Hunger For Your Grace
I Hunger For Your Mercy
And For Righteousness
I Hunger For Your Touch
I Hunger For Your Warm Embrace
I Hunger For Your Word, Your Voice
To See You Face To Face
To Stand In Your Presence
Engulfed In Holiness
Oh, Lord, I Hunger For You

I Hunger For You, I Hunger For You Lord
I Hunger For You, Hunger For You
Hunger For Your Love

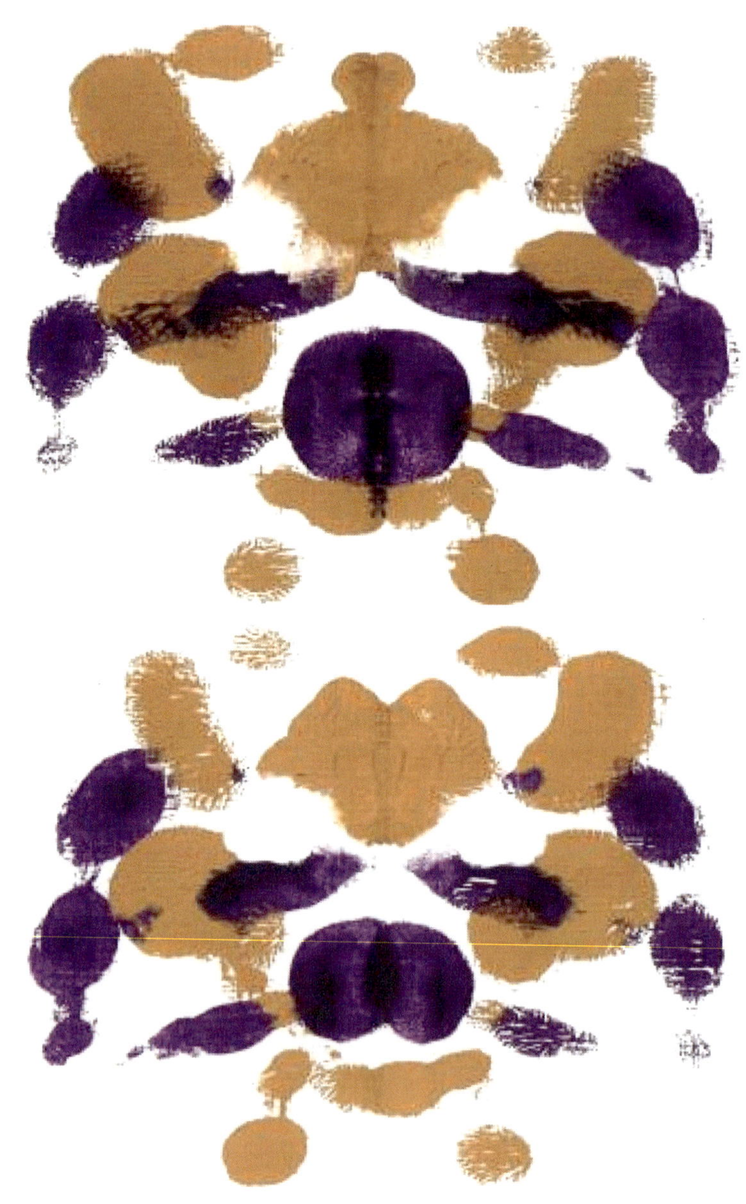

BOUNDARIES

You've Set Many Boundaries For Yourself Protecting Your Heart From
Feeling Hurt And Pain
You've Boxed Yourself In Such A Small Space, Limiting Your Dreams
Your Visions, And Shortening Your Reach

God Has So Much More In Store, He Wants You To Grow Beyond The
Limits Of Your Mind.
There's Increase And Overflow Of Blessings, Breakthrough Of
Your Self-Placed Boundaries
See You As God Sees You, Look Beyond Your Boundaries And See God
Try Him And See

It's Not That Hard To Look Beyond Your Self-Made Boundaries
Just Open Your Heart And Mind To The Father And Look Upon Yourself
As You Live In This Life, Just As God Sees And Has Designed It Just For You

Trust Him And Walk In Your Faith, For The Lord Our God Wants You To Prosper
He Wants To Bless Everything That Your Hands Shall Touch And Bless
Everywhere Your Feet Shall Trod

So Now, You Have A Choice To Make, What Will Be Your Next Move?

I LIVE

I Know That I'm Alive Because Of The Air That I Breathe
The Blood That Flows Within Me, A Gift So Precious You So Freely Give
Despite Of All The Wrongs I've Done

You Forgave Me And You Cleansed My Retched Soul That I May Have
Everlasting Life That's How I Know That I'm Alive
It's In You That I Live

Bread Of Life, Bread Of Heaven
I Shall Never Hunger Again
Precious Fountain, Living Water
I Shall Never Thirst Again
You're The One True Vine
The Fruit Of Life
I Live For You

That's How I Know That I'm Alive
I Live Because Of You, It's In You That I Live

MY HEART'S PRAYER

Hear My Prayer, Lord
Hear My Prayer, Oh Lord, My Heart Is Longing For You
I Need You, I'm Calling Out To You, To Fill My Heart With Your Holy Spirit
I'm Longing For Your Holiness, I Want To Be Transformed By You
Oh Lord, This Is My Heart's Prayer To You

For You To Be Proud
Of The Things I Do And Say
For You To Dance With Me
When I See You Face To Face
The Thought Of Hearing Your Voice Saying
I'm So Very Proud Of You
Is My Heart's Desire
Please Hear My Prayer

This Is My Heart's Prayer

Hear My Prayer, Lord
Hear My Prayer, Oh Lord, My Heart Is Longing For You
I Need You, I'm Calling Out To You To Fill My Heart With Your Holy Spirit
I'm Longing For Your Holiness, I Can Only Be Transformed By You
Oh Lord, This Is My Heart's Prayer To You

For You To Take Me By My Hand
As I Spread My Wings And Soar
For You To Walk With Me
Even Just To Show Me Your Throne
The Thought Of Being Held By You
And To Feel Your Warm Embrace

Is My Heart's Desire
Oh Lord, Hear My Prayer

This Is My Heart's Prayer
Hear My Prayer, Oh Lord

I'm Longing For Your Holiness, I Long To Be Transformed By You
Oh Lord, This Is My Heart's Prayer To You

For My Name To Be Branded
In Your Holy Golden Scrolls
For You To Share With Me
All The Secrets Untold
The Thought Of Laying At Your Feet
Curled Up On Your Robe
Is My Heart's Desire
God Hear My Prayer
This Is My Heart's Prayer

This Is My Heart's Prayer
My Heart's Desire, Yeah
Hear My Prayer, Lord

Trust In Him

Trust In The LORD With All Thine Heart; And Lean Not Unto Thine Own Understanding

Proverbs 3:5

Often Time Life Will Cause You To Wonder
"Oh My God, Are You For Real... Lord, Why Me?"
"Why Is This Happening? Why Has That Happened?"
Or, "How In The World Could This Be?"

We Question God, We Cry, We Fuss
And Some Of Us May Cuss And Scream
While All Along We Stand In Awe
Looking Around In Disbelief

We Search For Answers Within And Without
Looking To Ease Our Pain And Doubts
We Try And Try To Understand
How Could This Be In God's Perfect Plan?

Beloved, I Know For I Once Was There
And That Is Why I Am Here To Share
Look At His Word, Read It And Believe It
Trust In The Lord, Believe Me, He Cares

We Cannot Understand What All Happens In This Life
Please Be Careful Not To Develop Hatred Or Strife
For What The Devil Meant For Evil, God Has A Different Plan
He Will Turn It For Your Good And He Will Help You To Stand

What's In Store For You, Beloved, That I Don't Know
But God, With Time, His Plan, He Will Show
One Thing That I Have Learned And I Tell You No Lie
That Blessings Often Comes From The Pain Inside

So Seek His Face, His Knowledge And His Wisdom
And I'm Praying For You, Praying That Your Trust Be In Him

Be Patient

Be Ye Also Patient; Stablish Your Hearts: For The Coming Of The Lord Draweth Nigh.
James 5:8

I Know Life Has Given You Quite A Tumble
Causing Your Heart To Groan And Grumble
Your Pain Is Real And That's No Doubt
I See Your Tears And I Hear Your Shouts
You May Not Want To Hear Me Say
But Things Will Get Better With Each Day
If You Trust His Word And Walk In Faith
Believe With Patience, It's Worth The Wait
I Know It's Hard When It's In Your Face
But Trust That God Is On The Case
It's Not Clichés That I'm Here To Share
It's The Love Of God Who Really Cares
I'm Here For You But Understand
God Is The One To Help You Stand
Until That Day That He Will Provide
All That Our Hearts Have Prayed Inside

Hold On

Hold On, Hold On, My Brother
Hold On, Just A Little While Longer
Look, Before You Know It Everything Will Be Alright, A Change Is Nearing
So Just Hold On
Hold On

Hold On, Hold On, My Sister
Hold On, Just A Little While Longer
Look, Before You Know It Everything Will Be Alright A Change Is Nearing
So Just Hold On
Hold On

My Brother, My Sister
You Gotta Ride On, Pray On, Sing On, March On, Fight On

Hold On, Just A Little While Longer
Before You Know It, I Believe You Will See It So, Hold On, Just Hold On

Trust And Believe That You'll See That Your Work Is Not In Vain
So Just Hold On

Hold On, Much Love To You, Now, You Hold On

All Things Are Possible

Jesus Said Unto Him, If Thou Canst Believe, All Things Are Possible To Him That Believeth.
Mark 9:23

Your Time Is Now Here, So Lend Me Your Ear
I Know It's Been Said, But A Path Has Been Laid
A Journey That's New For You To Go Through
One God Designed Just For You
You Were Created For A Reason, Shown Gifts In Due Season
Groomed For The Task, So Now You Must Act
Don't Be Afraid, God Will Direct Your Way
Trust And Believe And Don't Forget To Pray
Many Questions Will Come And Doubt Will Come Too
But Have Faith In Your Heart And Remember What's Been Taught
All Things Are Possible To Them That Believe
Now Walk In Faith And Let God's Spirit Lead

Rise Up

And Now I Stand And Am Judged For The Hope Of The Promise Made Of God, Unto Our Fathers.
Acts 26:6

It's Time For You To Rise And Stand
To Hear God's Voice, Take His Command
Walk By Faith And Not By Sight
For What Is Promised, You Will Have To Fight

Past Mistakes You've Made Are Gone
God Forgives You, A Chosen One
To Be An Example Of His Living Word
Of Grace And New Mercies; Love Undeterred

Prayer And Intercession Is In The Air
For Open Windows And Doors, Declared
That No Man Can Shut Although They Will Try
To Kill Your Belief And To Call You A Lie

Just Press Your Way Forward With Your Eyes On The Prize
For God Is With You And That Can't Be Denied
And Then You Will See On That Marvelous Day
The Manifestation Of The Promise Displayed

Try Him And See

Delight Thyself Also In The LORD: And He Shall Give Thee The Desires Of Thine Heart.
Psalm 37:4

There Is Something That Is On Me That I Need To Say
And I Pray That You Don't Mind And You Will Hear Me Today
I See Much Potential Hidden Within You
And I Thank God And Pray That It All Proves True
For I See His Angels Glowing In Your Light
Singing "Trust In The Lord, Make Him Your Delight."
His Arms Are Strong And They Are Opened Up Wide
He Is Wanting To Show You All That He Will Provide
He'll Supply Your Needs But That's Just A Part
For He Will Also Give You The Desires Of Your Heart
If You'll Seek His Face And His Love, Not Man's
Then He Will Show You That He Has The Best Plan
"How Do You Know?" You're Probably Thinking
Well, He Did It For Me And That's Why I'm Saying

Read His Word, Try Him And See
Then He Will Show That He Is Just That Sweet

There Is A Plan

"For I Know The Plans I Have For You," Says The Lord, "They Are Plans For Good And Not For Disaster, To Give You A Future And A Hope."
Jeremiah 29:11 NLT

The Spirit Of The Living God Has Place You In My Heart
And There Is A Word That I Would Like To Impart
Throughout My Day You Were On My Mind
And I Began To Pray Each And Every Time
Thinking About What's All In Store
Break Through, Miracles And So Much More
You See, God Is Working On Your Behalf
Helping You Get Past The Devil's Traps
God Know The Plans He Has For You
So Trust And Believe And Praise Your Way Through
And Then You Will See As Time Goes By
The Shower Of Blessings Released From On High
So Cast Your Cares Upon The Lord
For He Cares For You And So Do I

THE RACE

It's Time For The Race, Ready, Set, Go!
Run-Run-Run! Screams The Crowd, Run-Run-Run!
But What They Don't Know Is That You're Not Here To Be The Fastest
Racer Or Even Here To Win

No, You Have A Point To Prove To Yourself That You Can Reach
The Finish Line And Still Be Able To Stand On Your Feet
With God On Your Side Holding You Upright, Know That He'll Keep You
From Falling And He Is At Your Side

Run-Run-Run, They All Chant, Run-Run-Run
Press Your Way, Fight Through The Pain And Make It To The End
Let God Be Your Strength, Let Him Have Your Back. He's Leading And
Guiding You, He's Growing And Training You

Run-Run-Run, Push-Push-Push, Pray-Pray-Pray Your Way Through
You Can Make It To The End Cause God And His Angels Are Cheering For You
So Just Keep Moving And Remember That Your Victory Is Not Predicated
Upon The Number That You've Placed At The End Of The Race
Your Victory Is On The Fact That You've Endured To The End And That
You've Finished The Race
So Run Your Race At Your Pace And Finish
You Got This

BE STRONG

Only You Be Strong And Very Courageous That You May Do According
To All Of The Words That I Have Spoken Unto You

Dreams And Visions, I Have Shared With You, All That I Have In Store
That You May Prosper In All that You Do

So Be Strong, Courageous; Don't Be Afraid Just Be Vigilant
Knowing That I Am With You Wherever You Go, So Go-Go-Go-Go-Go-Go

Trust In Me For My Word Is True, Believe That I Will See You Through
All Things Are Possible If You Trust In Me
And Believe In You

Don't You Be Dismayed If You Should Stumble, Refocus And Keep Your
Mind On Me, I Will Guide You If You Put Your Faith And Trust In Me

You're Forgiven For I Have Chosen You, I Believe That Your Heart Is True
Know That I Love You And I'll Always Be There

So Be Strong, Courageous; Don't Be Afraid, Just Be Vigilant
Knowing That I Am With You Wherever You Go, So Go-Go-Go-Go-Go-Go

Trust In Me For My Word Is True, Believe That I Will See You Through
All Things Are Possible If You Trust In Me
And Believe In You

I Am The Lord Your God
And I Am With You Wherever You Go So Trust In Me
And Believe In You

Be Strong And Go

SO AMAZINGLY

When This World Was Bringing Me Down And I Was Hurting Inside
You Came And Spoke To Me Confirming The Path That God Has For Me
Speaking Life Into My Heart, Just As Iron Sharpens Iron
Strengthening Me To Push Through The Storm Despite What's Blown And Toss Away

So Amazingly
Truly A Servant Of God, Humbly Walking
Speaking So Sweetly Allowing His Message To Flow
As You Walk With Life In Authority
A Beauty From Above You Are

May God Bless Your Loving Heart

I Thank You
For The Blessed Soul That You Are
God Bless You
For The Spirit Controlling Your Heart
I Love You
For The Light Of God That Shines, You Bring
Reminds Me Of The Love God Has For Me

So Amazingly
Truly A Servant Of God, Humbly Walking
Speaking So Sweetly Allowing His Message To Flow
As You Walk With Life In Authority
A Beauty From Above, You Are

May God Bless Your Loving Heart

GOD GOT MY BACK

Ah—Uh... Hum... Woo,
Yeah-Yeah—Yeah-Yeah—Yeah-Yeah
Ah—Uh... Hum... Woo... Hoo,
Thank Ya, Lord—Thank Ya, Lord—Thank Ya

Ah—Uh... Hum... Woo
I Got A Testimony
Ah—Uh... Hum... Woo... Hoo
Let Me Tell My Story

The Devil Came After Me Yawl, He Tried To Take Me Out
Attack Me In My Body And My Home, Tried To Taint My Soul
But The Lord Reminded Me Of All The Things That He Has Done For Me.
God Is Turning It All Around For Me, Yeah So, You Know I'm Glad Above
All Things That, Woo, He Got My Back
Ah—Uh... Hum, Woo, So Glad, God Got My Back!

Ah—Uh... Hum... Woo,
Yeah-Yeah—Yeah-Yeah—Yeah-Yeah
Ah—Uh... Hum... Woo... Hoo,
Thank Ya, Lord—Thank Ya, Lord—Thank Ya

Ah—Uh... Hum... Woo
I Got A Testimony
Ah—Uh... Hum... Woo... Hoo
Let Me Tell My Story

Life Changed In All Sort Of Ways, Seemed Like It Was At An End
My Money Got Funny And My Change Strange, Then That Devil Started

Over Again
Problems With My Family And Friends, I Cried Lord Jesus, Please Enter In
He Said There's A Plan So Don't Be Afraid, I Started Remembering Him
Then I Saw Again That, Woohoo, He Got My Back

Ah—Uh... Hum... Woo
Yeah-Yeah—Yeah-Yeah—Yeah-Yeah
Ah—Uh... Hum... Woo... Hoo
Thank Ya, Lord—Thank Ya, Lord—Thank Ya

Ah—Uh... Hum... Woo
I Got A Testimony
Ah—Uh... Hum... Woo... Hoo
Thank Ya For Lettin Me Tell My Story

Ah—Uh... Hum... Woo
Yeah-Yeah—Yeah-Yeah—Yeah-Yeah
Ah—Uh... Hum... Woo... Hoo
Thank Ya, Lord—Thank Ya, Lord—Thank Ya

I'm So Glad That God, He Got My Back

I SHALL NOT BE MOVED

I Shall Not, I Will Not, No, I Shall Not Be Moved
Just Like A Tree That's Planted And Rooted Deep By The Water
I Shall Not Be Moved

I Shall Not, I Cannot, No, I Shall Not Be Moved
On Christ The Solid Rock Grounded Firmly In The Earth I Stand
I Shall Not Be Moved

I Shall Not Be Moved
Though I May Cry And Scream At What Tries To Kill My Dream
No Matter What Comes My Way Or How Bad It Seem
I Shall Not Be Moved

I Shall Not Be Moved
By The Dark Clouds That Come In The Storm And Rain
Or The Trials And Tribulations In Life That Brings Sorrow And Pain
I Shall Not Be Moved

I Shall Not Be Moved
By The Strong Waves And The Current Of The Sea
Or The Blowing Winds Turning About Trying Its Best To Break Me
I Shall Not Be Moved

I Shall Not Be Moved
I Shall Not Sway Away Until The Day I Come To See My Fate
With The Shining Of The Son In View At Heaven's Gate
I Shall Not Be Moved

I Shall Not Be Moved
With Jesus As My Captain, Leading And Guiding Me In His Light
I Can Renew My Faith And Regain Strength As I Continue This Fight
I Shall Not Be Moved

I Shall Not, I Will Not, No, I Shall Not Be Moved
Just Like A Tree That's Planted And Rooted Deep By The Water
I Shall Not Be Moved

I Shall Not, I Cannot, No, I Shall Not Be Moved
On Christ The Solid Rock Grounded Firmly In The Earth I Stand
I Shall Not Be Moved

THE GLORY OF THE LORD

The Glory Of The Lord Is My Strength. The Glory Of God Is My Grace. So, I Will Forever Praise His Name

The Glory Of The Lord Is My Joy. The Glory Of God Calms Every Storm
So I Will Forever Praise His Name

He Is My Refuge, My Strong Tower
He Is My Healing Power. He Is The Faith That I Hold On To. He Is The Peace That Soothe My Soul

Oh, The Glory Of The Lord Is My Strength And My Grace
That's Why I Shall Forever Praise His Name

Yes, The Glory Of The Lord Is My Strength
The Glory Of The Lord Is My Joy
Oh, How The Glory Of The Lord Gives Power To My Soul

His Grace Is Sufficient For Me, For His Power Is Made Perfect In My Weakness
The Lord Is My Strength And My Song; An Everlasting Rock For Me

So I'm Gonna Praise His Name, Yes, I'm Gonna Praise His Name
And Give Him Glory
I'm Gonna Praise His Name, Yes, I'm Gonna Praise His Name
And Give Him Honor
I'm Gonna Praise His Name, Yes, I'm Gonna Praise His Name
For He Is Worthy

And I Shall Forever Praise His Name, Always

Oh, The Glory Of The Lord Is My Strength And My Grace
That's Why I Shall Forever Praise His Name

MY GUARDIAN ANGEL

The Time Has Come, Your Number Was Called
Now You're Gone Away To A Better Place

It's Still Hard For Me Because I, So Selfishly
Want You To Stay Here With Me

To Feel Your Touch, Your Kiss While You're Holding Me
To Hear Your Voice Saying
"I Love You; Now Live Joyously In Victory."

I Miss Your Smile, Your Laughter And All Of Your Crazy Ways

The Hidden Nuggets Of Wisdom When Telling A Story Just To Brighten
My Day

The Way You Would Calm My Anxiety When Storms Came My Way
I Don't Want To Let You Go

My Guardian Angel, Watching Over Me
You're My Guardian Angel Now

But I Know You'll Become One Of That Number
Called Home To Stand At His Feet

You'll Wear A Crown Of Glory, Showing
How Much He's Pleased

You'll Receive Your Wings Of Honor, Showing His Love, As You Soar
Throughout The Heavens

Watching Over Me

I Know, I Can See It, Oh I Believe It, I Can Hear You Singing All Around Me Now

"Holy-Holy; Glory-Glory
How Excellent Is Our God!

Hallelujah To The Lord God Almighty

How Sovereign Is Your Name!
The Great I Am,
How You Reign Upon Your Throne"

Watching Over Me

I Love You
My Guardian Angel, You're Always There, And You Keep Watching Over Me

Thank You

COME SOAR

These Flowers That I Give To You Today Is Simply To Express What Words Cannot Say
The Love You Gave To Me Is Hard To Define, The Unconditional Terms That Our Love Should Imply
You Shared Wisdom, You Shared Your Knowledge, And With All Of The Lessons That You've Taught To Me
Is The Very Reason That God Forever Show His Heart To Me

Know My Understanding Now Is There And All The Things That I Do Are Done In Love And Care
You've Helped Me Grow And To Be Well Equipped For
The Harsh Realities Of This Life So I Won't Quit
This Was All Done To Show You Love Me And You've Seen All That I Can Be
But Best Of All You'll Know That When Your Time Has Come To An End
You'll Hear God Say To You

Well Done My Child, The Race You've Won, Come Into My Kingdom

Enter In My Friend, Welcome Home My Love. Here's Your Wings, Come Soar Next To Me

Here's Your Wings, Spread Your Wings
Come And Soar Next To Me

HOW YOU LOVE ME

God, You Looked Passed My Flaws And All My Weaknesses
You Looked Beyond Every Single One Of My Faults
You Saw My Needs And Blessed Me So
It's Hard For Me To Apprehend How Much You Love Me Or Even How Deep That Love Flows
How You Sent Your Son To Make That Ultimate Sacrifice
Just To Set Me Free

The Thought That You Would Take The Time Just To Hold Me In Your Arms
The Thought That You Would Take The Time To Sing Me A Song
Just To Show Me How Much You Care And That You're Always There
I'm Amazed At How You Love Me, Unconditionally
You Love Me

Who Am I That You Thought It Right To Shed His Blood For Me
Who Am I That You Would Stretch Out Your Hands Just To Catch My Falling Soul

You've Changed Everything Within Me, Renewing My Life, Making Me Whole Again
Your Love Is Amazing And My Soul Sings Out To You

Oh-Oh-Oh-Oh, Oh
Hallelujah, Majestic Holy God
Oh-Oh-Oh-Oh, Oh
How Excellent Is Your Sovereignty
Oh-Oh-Oh-Oh, Oh
Precious, Phenomenal Deity

You're Truly Amazing,
Thank You For Loving Me

HE IS GOD

I Delight Myself In God Who Crafted Me With Love And Care
He Created Me, A Precious Jewel Found To Be Both Rare And Fair
With His Hands He Molded Me, In His Image I Was Meant To Be
To Glorify Him And To Call On Him By The Power Of His Name

For He Is The Great I Am, Yes, He Is God

Confidence, I Have In Myself For He Has Confidence In Me
To Do My Best In Everything And To Walk In My Authority
By The Power Of His Might He Blew The Breath Of Life In Me
To Live Life In His Light Courageously And Obediently

For He Is The Great I Am, Yes, He Is God

He Washed Me Clean, Anointing Me With The Oil Of All His Majesty
Sending The Comforter To Abide Within Me As His Angels Are Protecting Me
He Made Me, A Chosen One, For That, I Stand Strong And Tall
I Speak In Truth And Walk By Faith Knowing He'll Answer My Prayerful Call

For He Is The Great I Am, Yes, He Is God

For He Is And Will Always Be
Adonay (Lord, Master)
Elohim (God, Mighty Creator)
El Olam (The Eternal God)
El Shadday (God Almighty)

For He Is The Great I Am, Yes, He Is God

He Is, Abba (Father)
El Chay (Living God)
El Elyon (God Most High)
Yahweh (Lord)

For He Is The Great I Am
Yes, He Is God

YOU'RE THE REASON

You're The Reason That My Heart Beats Daily
Why I Rise And Look Up To The Son
I'm So Thankful For Your Loving Hands, Oh God

You're The Only Reason For Me

For My Heart Beats For You As The Blood Flows Through Me
With Every Breath I Take I'm In Awe Of You
I'm So Thankful For The Love You Share
You're The Reason, My Only Reason

Yes, You're The Reason That My Heart Beats Daily
Why I Rise And Look Up To The Son
I'm So Thankful For Your Loving Hands
Forever Thankful For Your Loving Hands, Oh God

You're The Reason, The Only Reason For Me To Be

Thank You, Father